# Winter in Halifax

# Winter in Halifax

Poems by

Thomas DeFreitas

Cover design by Shay Culligan

Cover photograph by Josh Hild
(unsplash.com/@joshhild)

ISBN: 978-1-63980-042-1

Kelsay Books
502 South 1040 East, A-119
American Fork, Utah 84003
Kelsaybooks.com

*for Hilary Sallick*
*and Mary Buchinger*
*my big sisters in poetry*

# Acknowledgments

Below, a listing of the poems in this collection that have been published in magazines, anthologies, and online journals. In many cases, the poems appeared in an earlier, slightly different version.

*Dappled Things:* "Lorca"

*Ibbetson Street:* "Our Lady of Cambridge"

*Muddy River Poetry Review:* "That Tall Tree" (as "Of That Tall Tree")

*On and Off the Road: Poems of New Hampshire:* "Franconia" (as "Summer 1980" and "What Mom Thought of My Franconia Poem")

*Plainsongs:* "Chasing the Waves," "Detox," "The Old Dry Dock," "Winter in Halifax"

*Red Letter Poems:* "Lingua Franca" (Poems for RLP are chosen and electronically circulated by Arlington, MA Poet Laureate Steven Ratiner)

*Somerville Times:* "Mandarin"

*Soul-Lit:* "Divorces," "Letter to Elena" (as "86th Letter to Elena"), "Women of Newfoundland" (as "Newfoundland")

*The 2017 Poetry Marathon Anthology:* "Reading Hart Crane" (as "Hart Crane")

I would like to thank Karen Kelsay, Delisa Hargrove, and all at Kelsay Books for their kindness, their knowledge, their attention, their availability, and their courtesy. Thanks to Shay Culligan for his design of the cover, and to Josh Hild for his photograph which mirrors—by happy chance—the scene and mood of the title poem.

Thanks also to Wayne-Daniel Berard, Bill Chatfield, Harris Gardner, Doug Holder, Caitlin Jans, Meredith McCann, Zvi A. Sesling, Eric Tucker, and Laura Marvel Wunderlich, editors whose publications have welcomed several of these poems.

Illimitable gratitude to Mary Buchinger, Hilary Sallick, Linda Haviland Conte, and everyone I know through the New England Poetry Club, not forgetting the late Victor Howes. I owe an unrepayable debt to Miriam Levine, to Cathie Desjardins, and to Steven Ratiner, past and present poets laureate of Arlington, Massachusetts, for their encouragement and example. And no litany of thanksgiving would be complete without mentioning Elena Lee Johnson of Milwaukee, whose alert, sensitive, and supremely accomplished poems inspire me always.

Loudest of shout-outs to Debba, Heather, Lisa, Jim, Alisha, Karen, Donna, Steven, John, Ingrid, Don, Sue, Naomi, Acadia, Carol, Sam, and Ed. And yes, Jen, you luminous soul, keep sending down your shining light. To all my buddies at the Manor: you rock! And blessings to everyone at "138": the Cathedral Church of Saint Paul (Episcopal) on Tremont Street in Boston.

I rejoice perpetually in my family. Mom, big hug, and boatloads of love. Dad, keep an eye on me from up there! Aunts and uncles and cousins, you have encouraged me mightily. I cherish you all.

Peace and light.

# Contents

# Winter in Halifax

I'm just riding the Happiness Express
with a suitcase full of tatterdemalion language:
defaulted loans be damned, I need a stiff drink
and a maritime gal of brass-knuckled laughter.

Dejection, scrammez-vous! Bad mood, begone!
I'd rather be plastered in Halifax this winter
than sober in Schenectady. Take me back
to the dive bars, the scruffy pubs of yesteryear!

The Happiness Express pulls into Halifax
at 4:06 in the morning; sleepless among
stray walkers in the cold, a black Lab
is baying at the glacially setting moon.

Nothing's open for business: no museum,
no bakery, no bookstore, no internet café—
but I'm as light-hearted as a florist in February
to be in the Halifax of gin-soaked valentines.

# Our Lady of Cambridge

Virgin of Harvard Square, gendering grace,
watch over Holyoke Center, the Garage,
Chameleon Tattoos, and the nose-ring place.

Pray for the pink-haired waif of mournful face
and ink-sleeves on both ghost-white arms. Take charge
(Mother of winter roses blushing with grace)

of Raven, Grendel's, Peet's; and, just in case,
tend to hungry undergrads at the large
Palace of Pizza near the nose-ring place.

Keep the Yard safe and sage. Make it your space.
Send down, *María,* pardon from the stars;
expand this city's heart! Lady of grace,

shelter the sleepers crouched in church doorways
against the cold; protect the crowds in bars,
the punks in the Pit and at the nose-ring place.

Gather us all in your clement embrace;
hasten with healing for our wounds and scars.
Bless Newbury Comics, bless the nose-ring place,
spare-change Madonna, prodigal of grace!

# The Old Dry Dock

It's ninety-five degrees at three o'clock,
and humid as New Orleans in the Hub.
A boozy Monday. Whiskey, classic rock.

Acadia keeps 'em comin' as we talk
baseball and politics. Cool in the pub,
but ninety-five outside at three o'clock.

She tells a sloppy lush, *Hey, take a walk.*
He mouths off on the way out. Poor schlub,
blasted after shots and '70s rock.

St. John's Episcopal was on this block.
Closed down for good. There's a gay nightclub
a street or two away. By four o'clock

some regulars at Boston's Old Dry Dock
go home to bed, to couch, to cold white tub
after a day of hooch and gray-haired rock.

Professor, call girl, clergywoman, jock
rub elbows with poet and cop. This sub-
terranean West End dive turns back the clock
with "Fat Bottomed Girls" and "Crocodile Rock."

# Vesperal

I would preserve
the sun's dim glow
of a February afternoon
muffled and gray
when the sky weighs down
with soon-coming snow

I would immortalize
the electric light
of my humble kitchen
where I've made coffee
which I sip so late
as I sit and write

I would offer a psalm
to the dark-garbed mood
of a day all dusk
when memory takes hold
and all a soul can do
is sigh and brood

I would intone an ode
that looks toward lost days
and longs for what is not
but the phone rings
and breaks this heavy haze
of sad sweet thought

# Arch Street Candles

*Arch Street: the popular nickname among Boston-area Catholics for Saint Anthony's Shrine, the Franciscan friary at 100 Arch Street, Downtown Crossing, Boston, MA*

They're fake,
these candles by the saints' statues,
these electric flickers glassed in red plastic.

Red as the blood of martyrs:
Becket, Romero, good Saint Lawrence.
Red as the lettering
of old Latin rubrics.
Red as the strawberries
sold by fruit vendors on nearby Summer Street.

Red as the Downtown Crossing subway sign.
Red as the dresses
in the red-light district.

Red as the Passion,
red as the Precious Blood,
red as the Five Wounds,
red as the Sacred Heart
exposed and blazing from the chest
against which the beloved disciple leaned.

Red as the nail-polish
on the toes of the Haitian housewife
plunking down her bundles with a heavy sigh
to station herself in a stiff wooden pew,
to take out her beads and whisper the Rosary
into the ear of the Queen of Heaven.

# Katie

Katie would listen
to sparrows preaching,
would swim in shimmering
heat with seagulls,
would gather pebbles
of many shapes and colors,
she'd puff away the seeds
of the bobbly dandelion.

Katie would laugh
at screwball comedies,
she'd pray to Jesus
in the old Italian church,
she'd walk barefoot
in damp June grass,
she'd speak French to kittens,
write poems to Chicago,
she'd scrutinize the ladybug
and bless the drenching rain.

Katie would sing
and play and breathe:
she'd hum and croon
with Joni Mitchell,
would lazily sway
through Carolina fields,
would let the wind
whip her long hair wild,
she'd joke with saints,
hold hands with sinners,
she'd banter with butterflies.
But that was before.

Katie was a grace.
A parcel of wonder,
a bundle of surprise.
But she married a man
with a heart like a fist
and that was the end
of the Katie I knew.

# Chasing the Waves

With Dad. Revere Beach, 1972.
My three-year-old legs would scurry to pursue
The beast of the Atlantic in retreat.

Of course, its watery paws would soon rush back
To maul the shore. I'd run from their attack
As quickly as I could on toddler feet.

Delighted, Dad would look on, and would shout
Encouragement and warning: "Hey, watch out!
They're gonna getcha!" I would shriek and laugh.

I'm older now than Dad was then. No son
To teach this excellent art of having fun,
Of chasing waves for an hour, or a half.

# 1978

There were two massive winter storms that year,
two weeks apart. The second, termed the Blizzard,
dumped feet of snow on the remnants of the first.

They took a month-long chunk out of third grade.
Our front door grudged to open, and the glass
of all our windows bore a brilliant frosting.

The governor addressed the public, wearing
a different sweater each day. The rest of us
discovered communion in our common lot:

walking in streets few cars could navigate,
wielding our shovels, building our snowmen,
searching for anyone who was selling milk.

Some coastal towns got ocean-water flooding
on top of snow and brutal winter wind.
Inland, a boy died, buried beneath the drifts.

A year older than me. Ten to my nine.
*Peter*. I remember his first name.

# She

She was Carmen Jones and "Killing Me Softly,"
the tents of Kedar and the curtains of Salma.
She was Charlie Parker and Lady Day,
the Nobel Prize, the Impossible Dream,
Michelangelo and the month of May.
She was Signed Sealed Delivered,
Blinded by the Light,
Betcha by Golly Wow.
She was Hammerin' Hank,
Earth, Wind & Fire,
bumblebees and baptism
and the wine of astonishment.
She ruled him like Britannia,
she laid him waste like Carthage.
Vesuvius and Venus,
Fra Lippo Lippi and the Three Degrees,
Sugar Pie Honey Bunch,
the Summer of Love:
she was all that.
She was Beatrice and Brooklyn,
Easter and ecstasy,
happiness and apple-blossoms.
She was Marvin Gaye and Tammi Terrell,
Pavarotti and *Purple Rain,*
an Ode to Joy and a Song of Praise.
She was All Hail the Queen,
she was Opposites Attract,
she was Black by Popular Demand.
She was coffee and the Cocteau Twins,
Death Be Not Proud and Do the Right Thing,
What's Goin' On and Fight the Power,
the Joyful Kilmarnock Blues.

She was the fall of the Wall,
the *Exsultet,* the *Magnificat,*
a Velvet Revolution
in living color.
She was the second martini
and the Third Glorious Mystery.
She was Ella singing Cole Porter,
she was under his skin but good.

# Reading Hart Crane

A rough-tongued winter.
Shell-trash and gull-clutter
along the dirty curve
of Revere Beach.
The Atlantic churns
its mass of liquid slate
with cold relentlessness.

The sixteen-year-old poet
carries a paperback
at least twice his age.
A yellowing Oscar
Williams anthology.

He reads the words
of the self-drowned psalmist
of tropic voyages,
Marlovian hymnographer
of azure deeps and steeps.

The sea claimed you,
Hart Crane, as you
claimed the sea, scribe
of brined bones,
of doom and spume,
the merciless ocean's
"bent foam and wave"
swallowing your song.

# Lorca

What do you dream of,
murdered magician?
Menace and moonlight,
the forest's million eyes.

Guitars of glass,
sapphire doves,
implacable flutes.

Green flesh of heaven.
Brown blood of earth.
Scarlet reputation
of Iberian roses.

Heart of the thundercloud,
white fire, diamond death.
Womb of the raindrop,
embryonic continent.

Far beyond the horizon,
beyond the spying stars,
urchins and virgins weep
tears scalding and barbed,
tears of Iscariot,
tears of the Magdalene.

Each thought a thorn
in the brow of a stylite.

Each night narcotic,
poison in the pulse.
Each day a threat,
a knife of ice.

# February Thaw

Amid stacked paperbacks, cold coffee-mugs,
on a snow-swept Thursday morning, I recite
the sun-soaked poem of your petalled name
to kitchen furniture, to plaster saints.

In tepid light I sit, graybearded bookworm
wishing your wine-bright voice would bring new life
to my frost-freaked heart. I listen for
your laughter, raucous liturgy of Spring!

The calendar approaches Lent, black badge
of ashes on pale foreheads, a grave priest
intoning *thou art dust* to solemn sinners:

but you, my fresh-fledged rose, my rush of rain,
unwinter me, frolic my sluggish blood
with mud-tongued songs and stumblefooted dances!

# My Dove in the Cleft of the Rock

Feed me with salmon cakes,
refresh me with peppermint tea,

offer me Glenmorangie
as we listen to Says You

on an old transistor radio
that works as good as new.

\*

Let me walk you home on those cold nights
when we've stayed out till the witching hour
talking Cole Porter and metaphysics.

Let me help you move
those big cardboard boxes
out to the recycle bin.

Let me be the pair of eyes
next to yours
looking up at Orion
in a clear black January sky.

Let me buy you clementines, walnuts,
boxes of Celestial Seasonings.

\*

I would dance with you
to songs that I croon
as we turn and sway;

I would sing for your delight
"When I'm Sixty-Four"
and "The Wonder of You."

I'd sing in Italian:
*io che non vivo*
*più di un' ora senza te …*

\*


Let me walk with you
the twelve blocks from Central Square
to Congregation Eitz Chayim
on Magazine Street
where services are Fridays at seven.

Let me be your shield
against startlement and shadow,
against menace and misery,
against all things dark and arctic.

\*


Let there be cider at the Kickstand Café,
music at the Highland Avenue Armory.
Let me hug and hold your slender form
made ample with winter sweaters.

# Blueberries in August

1.

My poetfriend Mary
visited Maine last week,
and went blueberry-picking.
She had gathered up
buckets of them,
deep blue parcels,
and wanted to share!
So, Monday morning,
I took a bus to her
neighborhood in Cambridge,
and I walked up to her porch
where, on a small round table,
she had placed a plastic bag
containing a pound,
maybe two pounds, of her harvest.
She waved hello
from her window
as I accomplished
the contactless pick-up.
And as she waved, I bowed
a deep bow of gratitude.

2.

Darker
than the brooding gentians
in Lawrence's poem,
velvety blue-black,
abundant, it seemed,
as stars
in a North Country sky.
Around the eye-holes
where the stems had been,
some berries had peeled a little,
revealing a subcutaneous
blush of pink.
I tasted them.
They were winsomely tart,
nothing spectacular at first,
but then they'd detonate
and the flavor would linger
as the heat of a summer day does
past dusk, well past dusk,
as a favorite song
lingers in the noggin
and you find yourself humming it
at odd moments,
as memories linger
in the hurt heart,
sweet memories
of loved ones
(Bangum, "the Bishop,"
and dearest Jen)
gone far, far too soon.

# Detox

A hurt woman of thirty, thirty-five,
doing a seven-day stint at Pine Grove detox
paces, hazy, puzzled to be alive:
feet wedged in flip-flops, sheathed in dirty socks.

Her voice is Castle Island, her first name
a common one for children of the '80s.
She clings to the few comforts of this Hades:
cigarettes, decaf coffee, shared shame.

Red-haired, her face all freckle and tear-streak,
familiar as Broadway or Andrew Station,
she manages both defiance and defeat.

I ponder the sad mystery of her feet
scuffing the Lysol'd halls of desolation
where she'll get sober if only for a week.

# Letter to Elena

Yesterday I wept for a lost friend,
who died some months ago in wise midlife:
a woman whose wit and counsel I cherished
and who succumbed to a quickly-spreading cancer.

Yesterday I had the good company
of your book in the eye doctor's waiting-room.
Your poems bring me the Illinois of your youth:
corn and sun, wide blue sky, and tender growth.

Yesterday I saw a woman of seventy
offering to help a woman of twenty-five
(whose fingers had been fumbling at the task)
bind her dark abundant hair
in a yellow ribbon.
The two were strangers, newly met
in the underground Harvard busway.
The younger woman crouched a bit
and suggested, "If you could make a bow?"
and the older woman did so, lovingly.

Yesterday I read of an elderly rabbi
climbing a chair during gunfire
to urge his terrified congregation
to immediate safety and to future courage.

Yesterday was Monday, full springtime.
April in New England is a festival,
a riot of blossoms, bright and bold,
that will not make it to the end of May.

# Franconia

*Summer 1980*

I hadn't yet begun at Latin School.
I hadn't yet met Mr. Waldron
or the poetry of Robert Frost.

But I had met the mountains of Franconia
the Old Stone Face overlooking the Notch,
dirt roads tucked among a myriad of evergreens,
placid two-lane state roads winding for miles.

I'd ride my yellow ten-speed down Magowan Hill,
under the interstate, up 18 to the center of town.

*The Hillwinds. The Franconia Public Library.*
*Our Lady of the Snows. Shop & Save.*
*The Dutch Treat. The Grateful Bread.*

There were August nights of forty-two degrees
with constellations of fireflies,
fitful bead-sized go-lights in the deep North Country dark.

The Old Man has crumbled and fallen to earth.
Mr. Waldron has been retired for years.
But Route 18 still goes from the north end of the Notch
up to Littleton, suburbanized, Walmarted,
lately bereft of the Village Book Store.

And the fireflies of my twelfth summer,
lucent dots of nuclear green against the thick nocturnal black,
doubtless have descendants more numerous
than the seed of Abraham,

bellies flickering in the woods and clearings
to dazzle the eyes of children:
these fireflies, these tiny mutant stars.

\*

*What Mom Thought of My Poem*

I liked it, but I wanted more.
Is there a way you could
add a few lines?

Tell people
how easygoing everybody is
in the North Country:
no traffic, no swearing,
no honking of horns.
Strangers say hello to you
when you're walking to the store.
That elderly couple who helped me
when I fell off the bike,
I'll never forget them.

You sleep better in the mountains.
And you have a bigger appetite!
Something about the fresh air
makes you famished.
After you spend the day
shopping or golfing or swimming,
you eat the legs off the table!

You get some big doozy thunderstorms!
I shouldn't be afraid of them after all these years.

It's a different way of life
than you'd find in East Boston.
Pine trees, lakes, rivers, peace and quiet.
If I could write poetry,
I'd let people know.

# Rouse for Roethke

Big Ted Roethke, what's his game?
He can buss the butterfly,
He can snow the blushing rose,
Call Dame Ladybug by name.

Count of creaturely delight,
He can herrick with the best:
Married to the wormy earth,
He's the swain of gladdest girth.

When he dances, Bedlam sings;
Lyric fingers pluck their strings:
Joyful bodies rub and budge
To his red-blood psalms of love.

Watch him garland up a page!
He's no mushroom, he's a sage!
He can coax the daffodil
With a single syllable.

*Theodore, my robust rhymer,*
*No one bards a garden finer!*
*You're the heir and princely son*
*Of Clare, Carew, and Campion.*

# That Tall Tree

Longfellow, can you tell me the name of that tall tree?
Will poets' ghosts invade the frame of that tall tree?

Cambridge is home to dozens, scores of churches:
Nuns pray to Mary, blessed dame of that tall tree.

Fresh-firecoal fall, ahoy! I cherish your brief weeks.
Leaves blush red, the shame of that tall tree!

Spring broadcasts lilac-rumors along the peopled banks
Of the Charles, spreads the fame of that tall tree.

Winter caps the hedges with a kippah of fresh snow:
Mittened children learn the game of that tall tree.

Butterflies dance, unfazed by loutish summer;
Metallic blue sky, you are the aim of that tall tree!

Sonneteer of Brattle Street, much-belaurelled,
Your verses keep it burning, the flame of that tall tree.

# You're Gone

You're gone, and life's a hole without a sock,
A fruitless rind, some coffee-grounds (no brew):
Sarcastic stars can only jeer and mock.

I miss those sun-touched hours we'd sit and talk,
When love was young, faith fresh, and hope brand-new:
You're gone, and life's a hole without a sock.

Alone in a cold flat at three o'clock,
I write my villanelle (all about you):
Cynical stars deride, condemn, and mock.

Whether I listen to Britpop, classic rock,
Broadway or jazz, it's all one shade of blue:
You're gone, and life's a hole without a sock.

I can't go back in time and take a walk
With the one delight I'd dare to label true:
Unsympathetic stars! why must they mock?

Dante's Italian and Arnaut's *langue d'oc*
Can't shape the praises that are your just due:
Merciless stars can sneer and snipe and mock—
You're gone, and life's a hole without a sock.

# Divorces

are never easy.
The lady barkeep, mid-thirties,
on whom I've had a hopeless crush
since the summer of 2010.
Ministering angel
of my Bowdoin Street watering-hole.

Knee-high boots and four-letter words
bruising the soul
like a fist of brass.

I want to clutch my pillow,
assume the fetal position,
and sob loud racking sobs.

I want to say my rosary on her toes.

I love her like Dylan Thomas
and autumn and Glenlivet
and breath and bread
and sweet suffering Jesus
and Thandie Newton's ankles.
I love her like St. Matthew's Passion
and "Come On, Eileen"
and the Luminous Mysteries.

I can't go there anymore.
And I think it's going to
hurt for a while.

# Lingua Franca

My language languishes:
it neither scampers nor frisks;
it executes no back-flips,
no handstands, no moonwalks;
my language does not somersault;
it does not pirouette;
it neither pounces like the cobra
nor springs like the yearling lamb.

I want that lithe and limber idiom,
that sassy brassy palaver,
that red-stiletto dialect,
that margarita-mother-tongue
with the salted rim,
spectacular vernacular,
slang with a bang;
I want blab, blurt, yawp, yelp,
hoot, howl, holler,
the *lingua franca*
of bump and tussle and nudge.

# Mandarin

Take the bright globe of the mandarin
from its red-mesh satchel in the fridge.
Slice the rind with a serrated knife,
three cuts making six acute angles.

Peel the skin to ravish its pulpy flesh.
Bite into a small curved wedge of the fruit,
cold as November, firm and yielding
as any gelatin. Let the juice, vital

with vitamins, burst against your palate:
each drop a festival of Miami revelry!
Take another wedge, and then another.
Offer mute exclamations of gratitude.

# Six in the Morning

Six in the morning. February. Coffee.
I stand at the cold porch door and look out on
the brooding sapphire of the foredawn sky
pregnant with deep blue light that pales and shines
toward the horizon, where the tops of trees
like scriptures in an inscrutable alphabet
imprint themselves on the margin of the day.

Stones in the neighboring graveyard
begin to whiten and become distinct;
traffic percolates through nearby streets:
sparrows sing crisp matins in the chill.

There is a gentle splendor in these hours
before the sun blares and commuters rush,
before St. Agnes' bells ring Angelus.

Yesterday marked the first day in a week
I did not see your face or hear your voice.

# Women of Newfoundland

Women are wise
in Newfoundland.
They speak sage words
with platinum blossoms
in their voices;
they sing bold songs
with sturdy earth
in each note.

Women are strong
in Newfoundland.
Rambunctious as oceans.
Philosophic as the stars.
With poems and power
in their unstumbling feet,
with Dante and divinity
in their fearless eyes,
with harp and psaltery
in the swooning curve
of their bellies.

Women are lively
in Newfoundland.
Spendthrift of mercy,
quick with justice.
Poetic as chartreuse,
intoxicating as twilight,
simple as astrophysics,
intricate as bread.

Women are real
in Newfoundland.
Legions of men
obey their eloquence.
Countless acolytes
heed their silence.
I hope you understand.
Women are beautiful
in Newfoundland.

# A Sunday in April

Everything was singing
near the Mystic River Parkway:
daffodils, crocuses,
pillows of white cloud
in a sky blue-bright,
fresh as laundry
drying on a clothesline.

Passers-by smiling
from behind
anti-viral masks.
You could see it in their eyes.

Blond dogs
straining at their leashes.

Bicyclists getting speed-bumped
by the roots of trees
along the well-worn path
of the riverbank.

Two canoeists
in one canoe
making their way
through peaceful water
at a lazy pace.

Joggers waving hello
as they pounded and panted
the unrelenting rhythm
of rain-or-shine fitness.

Couples holding hands—
heedless of hygienic distancing.

And on a park bench
beneath the wind-bowed branches,
a fellow of sixty-five, at least,
with a white handlebar mustache,
and a black cowboy hat—
he opened a case
and took out his guitar,
and began to strum
and croon *Hallelujah,*
*hallelujah.*

And truly, everything
stopped for a while,
caught its breath,
and listened.

# About the Author

Thomas DeFreitas was born in 1969 in Boston. He was educated at the Boston Latin School, and attended the University of Massachusetts (Boston and Amherst) for two years. His poems have appeared in *Dappled Things, Ibbetson Street, Muddy River Poetry Review, Pensive, Plainsongs, Soul-Lit,* and elsewhere.

In the spring of 2018, Thomas's poem "Chasing the Waves" was chosen by Arlington, Massachusetts Poet Laureate Cathie Desjardins to be part of the Talking Chair Project, an interactive poetry exhibit developed and designed by Emily Calvin-Bottis, and installed during National Poetry Month at the Robbins Library in Arlington. In the summer of 2019, "Detox" was chosen as an Award Poem by the editors of *Plainsongs.*

A resident of Arlington, MA since 2010, Thomas is a member of the Academy of American Poets, the New England Poetry Club, and Arlington's Bee Hive Poets.